U.S. HISTORY TIMELINES

Westward Expansion
1803-1900s

Steve Goldsworthy

www.av2books.com

AV² provides enriched content that supplements and complements this book. Weigl's AV² books strive to create inspired learning and engage young minds in a total learning experience.

Your AV² Media Enhanced books come alive with...

Audio
Listen to sections of the book read aloud.

Key Words
Study vocabulary, and complete a matching word activity.

Video
Watch informative video clips.

Quizzes
Test your knowledge.

Embedded Weblinks
Gain additional information for research.

Slide Show
View images and captions, and prepare a presentation.

Try This!
Complete activities and hands-on experiments.

...and much, much more!

Go to **www.av2books.com**, and enter this book's unique code.

BOOK CODE

L482427

AV² by Weigl brings you media enhanced books that support active learning.

Published by AV² by Weigl
350 5ᵗʰ Avenue, 59ᵗʰ Floor
New York, NY 10118
Websites: www.av2books.com   www.weigl.com

Library of Congress Control Number: 2014933464

ISBN 978-1-4896-0720-1 (hardcover)
ISBN 978-1-4896-0721-8 (softcover)
ISBN 978-1-4896-0722-5 (single-user eBook)
ISBN 978-1-4896-0723-2 (multi-user eBook)

Printed in the United States of America in North Mankato, Minnesota
1 2 3 4 5 6 7 8 9 0   18 17 16 15 14

052014
WEP301113

Project Coordinator: Aaron Carr
Editor: Pamela Dell
Designer: Mandy Christiansen

Every reasonable effort has been made to trace ownership and to obtain permission to reprint copyright material. The publishers would be pleased to have any errors or omissions brought to their attention so that they may be corrected in subsequent printings.

Weigl acknowledges Getty Images as its primary image supplier for this title.

CONTENTS

Before Expansion

At the beginning of the 1800s, the United States was a growing nation. The country had bought much land in the Louisiana Purchase. This purchase doubled the size of the country overnight. Now the country was working to settle exactly where its borders between Canada and Mexico would lay.

The United States was also struggling with the issue of slavery at this time. Another concern was the country's relationship with American Indians. The British supported the American Indians in their fight against U.S. **expansion**. This later led to war between the United States and Great Britain.

EXPLORERS BLAZED NEW trails into the West during the 1800s. Lewis and Clark had help as they explored the Northwest. A young Shoshone woman named Sacajawea was their guide. She helped them communicate with tribes along the way.

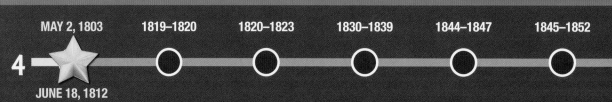

LOUISIANA PURCHASE

On May 2, 1803, the United States signed a **treaty** and paid France a total of $27,267,622 for 828,000 square miles (2 million square kilometers) of land between the Mississippi River and the Rocky Mountains. The territory stretched from the Gulf of Mexico in the south to Canada in the north.

WAR OF 1812

The United States declared war on Great Britain on June 18, 1812. For three years, the Americans fought the British. They battled along the Atlantic coast, in the Great Lakes region, and elsewhere. The conflict had many causes, including trade disagreements and the U.S. push for land. The war set U.S. boundaries, but neither side could claim true victory. In Ohio, Indiana, and Illinois, many American Indian groups who had sided with the British were pushed out of their territories. This allowed settlers to move even farther west.

LEWIS AND CLARK EXPEDITION

In 1803, under President Thomas Jefferson, U.S. Army captain Meriwether Lewis and William Clark began exploring the West. They traveled to the Pacific Northwest looking for waterways that led to the Pacific coast. Lewis and Clark reached the Pacific Ocean on November 15, 1805. Their efforts opened the West for many other **pioneers**.

MANIFEST DESTINY

"Manifest Destiny" was a term first used by journalist John O'Sullivan in 1845. Those who believed in Manifest Destiny felt that American expansion was their God-given right. They felt it was their duty to spread American ideas and values to others, including American Indians and Mexicans.

Many Americans believed it was their destiny to teach their ways to these people. They used Manifest Destiny to justify taking land, killing American Indians, and forcing their religious beliefs on others.

A Nation Divided

In the early 1800s, tensions had begun to divide the northern and southern states. Those tensions were growing. The nation was split on the issue of slavery. People in the North generally opposed slavery and wanted to outlaw it in the new territories. However, slavery was a way of life in the South. Most Southerners felt slavery was necessary.

Hoping to settle the differences, Congress passed the Missouri **Compromise** on March 3, 1820. The compromise allowed two new states into the **Union**. One was slave-holding Missouri. The other was the free state of Maine. The compromise kept the number of free and slave-holding states equal, which both North and South demanded. The act further stated that all western territories lying north of Missouri's southern border would be free.

The **Transcontinental** Treaty was a land agreement between Spain and the United States. Also known as the Adams-Onís Treaty, it was signed in 1819. According to the treaty, Spain gave up all rights to Florida and the Pacific Northwest. In return, the United States agreed that Spain would control Texas. Southerners wanted any land gains to benefit slaveholders. The North continued to resist this idea.

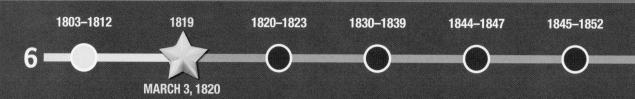

1803–1812 1819 1820–1823 1830–1839 1844–1847 1845–1852

MARCH 3, 1820

AMERICA'S ENSLAVED PEOPLE were considered property. They were always in danger of being beaten, sold, or even killed by their owners. Living conditions were poor as well, especially in the South.

The Race to Claim Land

In the 1820s, the United States continued to push its vision of Manifest Destiny. There was widespread belief in America's role, or destiny, to take over all land to the west. By doing so, the Americans meant to "save" the peoples living there. Controlling the West would also keep the land out of the hands of European rulers. Being ruled by kings, Americans knew, was not freedom.

The U.S. government especially wanted to claim land that European nations had not taken. The Americans of the 1800s felt it was their duty to claim this land before Great Britain or Spain did. By 1820, scores of settlers had built **frontier** towns as far west as the Mississippi River.

This push west continued to drive American Indians out of their homelands. Manifest Destiny was supposed to improve their lives. For thousands of people, however, life changed for the worse.

FOR MANY PEOPLE, manifest destiny was not the only reason for expanding to the west. The land to the west offered vast riches and resources just waiting to be claimed.

1803–1812   1819–1820   1820   1830–1839   1844–1847   1845–1852

DECEMBER 2, 1823

In the 1800s, many artists made artworks showing the United States as a beautiful woman. This woman, called Columbia, was usually shown as a large, angelic figure. She was often shown guiding settlers west.

THE MONROE DOCTRINE

On December 2, 1823, members of Congress heard President James Monroe's seventh annual State of the Union message. The statement declared that the United States would not allow any further **colonization** of the Western Hemisphere by European nations.

The Monroe Doctrine also sent a clear warning to foreign nations to not interfere in U.S. affairs. It was as close as the United States would come to making Manifest Destiny a law.

Trouble for American Indians

American Indians had lived on their lands for thousands of years. According to their beliefs, people could not own land. In the 1800s, however, the American settlers most certainly believed in land ownership, and they wanted more. Settlers claimed the land by purchase, treaty, or force. In the 1830s, the struggle between American settlers and American Indians grew worse.

The U.S. government wanted American Indian homelands in the East and South. They had tried using treaties to get five of the largest American Indian groups to move west. However, the American Indians would not go.

Finally, the government forced the issue. On May 28, 1830, Congress passed the Indian Removal Act. Under the laws of this act, President Andrew Jackson forced American Indians in the southeast to move onto **reservations** west of the Mississippi River. This led to years of suffering for American Indians.

THE INDIAN REMOVAL Act created reserved "Indian Territory." However, Americans later moved in and claimed this land as well.

The Trail of Tears

The Choctaw were the first American Indians forced to move under the Indian Removal Act. The journey was so terrible that one of the Choctaw chiefs called it a "trail of tears and death." From 1838 to 1839, thousands of Cherokee people were forced to move. In both cases, the American Indians faced extreme winter weather, food shortages, and other hardships. About 4,000 Cherokees died during the move. Today, the term "Trail of Tears" refers to the experience of all American Indians who were forced to move.

"It is with sorrow we are forced by the white man to quit the scenes of our childhood . . . We bid farewell to it and all we hold dear."

Cherokee Vice Chief Charles Hicks, November 4, 1838.

DURING THE TRAIL of Tears period, more than 100,000 American Indians were forced out of their homes.

The Oregon Territory

The United States, Great Britain, Russia, and Spain had all wanted control of the Oregon territory. This huge land area began at the northern border of California. It extended north to Alaska. It stretched west from the Rocky Mountains to the Pacific Ocean.

By 1844, with other countries out of the way, it was up to only the United States and Great Britain. Together, these countries had to decide boundaries and come to an agreement on claims to unsettled land in the Pacific Northwest. That year, James K. Polk won the presidency on his promise to expand U.S. territory. To avoid war, he suggested the **49th parallel** as the Oregon territory's northern border. Great Britain refused to this.

Tensions rose between the two countries. Great Britain, however, also wanted to avoid war. Before the conflict could reach that point, the British gave in. The border would be set at the 49th parallel, not including part of Vancouver Island.

THE 49TH PARALLEL agreement gave Puget Sound to the United States. For the Americans, this was a great advantage. From Puget Sound, in today's Washington State, the country could increase its trade with China and the Pacific Islands.

| 1803–1812 | 1819–1820 | 1820–1823 | 1830–1839 | 1844 | 1845–1852 |

In June 1846, pioneers headed west into the Sierra Nevada mountains. Led by a successful farmer named George Donner, the pioneers hoped to settle in California. Before they arrived, an early storm trapped them. Stranded for five months, the group, called the Donner party, ran out of food. Some survivors reportedly ate the dead to stay alive.

Today, California's Donner Pass is a reminder of that event. It is also recalls the challenges faced by early settlers of the American West.

THE DONNER PARTY was trapped in 5 feet (1.5 meters) of snow in the winter of 1846 to 1847. Continuing blizzards prevented escape. Out of 81 pioneers, only 44 survived.

The Mexican-American War

In December 1845, the U.S. government **annexed** the Republic of Texas. This made Texas a new American state, which caused tension with the Mexican government. The two countries did not agree on some areas of the Texas-Mexico border. President Polk felt that war was the only way to settle the matter.

On May 13, 1846, Polk declared war on Mexico. Many fierce battles followed, mainly in northeastern Mexico. After nearly two years, the war ended on February 2, 1848. Both sides signed the Treaty of Guadalupe Hidalgo. By this agreement, the United States paid $15 million for 525,000 square miles (1.4 million sq. km) of Mexican land. This included almost all of today's states of Arizona and New Mexico, as well as parts of present-day California, Utah, and other states.

AMERICAN TROOPS WON a great victory at the Battle of Buena Vista on February 23, 1847. They were led by Major General Zachary Taylor, who was elected president in 1848.

By late 1849, more than 100,000 people had entered California. These "forty-niners" were nearly all men. The gold rush brought more than 300,000 people into California. It was the largest movement of people in American history.

CALIFORNIA GOLD RUSH

On January 24, 1848, a mill operator named James W. Marshall found gold in northern California. He spotted the gold in the American River near Coloma. Word quickly spread. The California gold rush lured fortune hunters from across the nation. They also came from as far away as Europe, Australia, and China.

This rush of people into California led to widespread building of roads, towns, churches, and schools. With so much progress, California pushed for statehood. That goal was reached quickly, in 1850, By 1852, the gold rush was at its peak.

The Kansas-Nebraska Act

The Missouri Compromise of 1820 had outlawed slavery north of a line on maps known as the 36° 30' parallel. This northern region included today's state of Nebraska. Since slavery was illegal there, Southerners did not want the U.S. government to create a Nebraska territory.

To address this resistance, Congress passed the Kansas-Nebraska Act on May 30, 1854. The new law made matters worse, however. The act allowed settlers into both territories. Kansas lay in the "free state" area as well. The law ignored this fact. It gave settlers in Kansas the right to vote on whether that future state would allow slavery or not.

Northerners and Southerners flooded into Kansas by the thousands. By doing so, each side hoped to sway the vote on slavery in its own favor. Violent clashes broke out between the opposing sides. Things got so bad that the territory got the nickname "Bleeding Kansas." This clash was a hint of things to come. The United States was splitting apart.

DURING THE BLEEDING Kansas period, thousands of soldiers from both the North and South flooded into the state to fight over the issue of slavery.

1803–1812   1819–1820   1820–1823   1830–1839   1844–1847   1845–1852

SUPPORTING THE ACT

Illinois senator Stephen A. Douglas proposed the Kansas-Nebraska Act. Douglas wanted to build a coast-to-coast railroad that would pass through Chicago. He believed the new law would help make this happen.

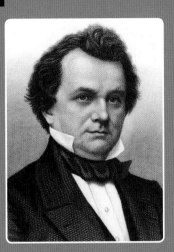

FIGHTING THE ACT

The new Republican Party was founded in 1854 by politicians who were against the Kansas-Nebraska Act. They wanted to end slavery in the United States. On November 6, 1860, Abraham Lincoln was elected president. He was the first Republican to lead the country.

When They Became States

Louisiana (18th state)
April 30, 1812

Missouri (24th)
August 10, 1821

Texas (28th)
December 29, 1845

Iowa (29th)
December 28, 1846

California (31st)
September 9, 1850

Minnesota (32nd)
May 11, 1858

Oregon (33rd)
February 14, 1859

Kansas (34th)
January 29, 1861

Nevada (36th)
October 31, 1864

Nebraska (37th)
March 1, 1867

Colorado (38th)
August 1, 1876

North Dakota (39th or 40th)
November 2, 1889

South Dakota (39th or 40th)
November 2, 1889

Montana (41st)
November 8, 1889

Washington (42nd)
November 11, 1889

Idaho (43rd)
July 3, 1890

Wyoming (44th)
July 10, 1890

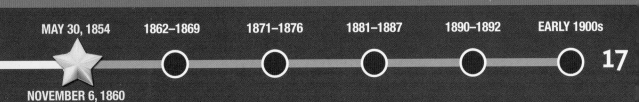

The Homestead Act

By 1862, the Civil War was raging. The North and the South were battling over the slavery issue. Eleven states had **seceded** from the Union. That same year, President Lincoln signed into law the Homestead Act.

The law took effect on May 20, 1862. It brought even faster settlement of the West. According to the act, settlers could take 160 acres (65 hectares) of government land. They would agree to improve the land by building a house on it. They also had to farm the land for at least five years. Then, for a small fee, they could own the property.

DURING THE CIVIL War years, few American men were available to help build the coast-to-coast railroad. Most were in combat.

1803–1812   1819–1820   1820–1823   1830–1839   1844–1847   1845–1852

Americans believed a cross-country railroad would strengthen and unite the country. To that end, Congress passed the Pacific Railroad Act on July 1, 1862. On January 8, 1863, work began in Sacramento on the Central Pacific Railroad. Chinese laborers made up more than 80 percent of the workforce.

Coming from the east, the Union Pacific railroad line met the western line at Promontory Summit, Utah, on May 10, 1869. There, the "last spike" was driven into the ground. The first transcontinental railroad was complete.

THE HOMESTEAD ACT allowed any U.S. citizen 21 years or older to claim land. Many families headed west to start a new life. Of the 4 million who filed land claims, only 40 percent fulfilled the requirements for keeping the land.

American Indian Resistance

After the Indian Removal Act of 1830, Americans swarmed westward. They quickly began taking over American Indian homelands. During the 1860s and 1870s, battles between settlers and American Indians were fierce and frequent. The American West was the site of hundreds of these conflicts.

By 1871, Congress had created 371 treaties with various American Indian groups. Many of these agreements forced the American Indians from their native homelands. Others appeared to present reasonable terms, but the Americans eventually broke the agreements.

ON JUNE 25, 1876, U.S. Lieutenant Colonel George A. Custer and 700 troops rode to the Little Bighorn River in Montana territory. They planned to clear the land of Sioux and Cheyenne American Indians camped there. Under the direction of Sioux Chief Sitting Bull, about 3,000 armed American Indians met them. Within three hours, Custer and 215 U.S. soldiers were dead.

1803–1812   1819–1820   1820–1823   1830–1839   1844–1847   1845–1852

Chief Sitting Bull was a proud warrior. He refused to leave his homeland in the Black Hills of Dakota. He said, *"If we must die, we die defending our rights."*

BREAKING THE FORT LARAMIE TREATY

The Fort Laramie Treaty of 1868 had given certain rights to the Sioux people. As part of this agreement, the Dakota Black Hills area was recognized as part of the Great Sioux Reservation.

In 1874, however, Lt. Col. Custer arrived in the Black Hills. Miners who had come with him found gold there. Eager to claim land, more Americans rushed in. This broke the Fort Laramie Treaty with the Sioux.

The Wild Frontier

The early American West was a wild **frontier**. Rugged men lived in rough conditions as towns sprung up across the land. Gun battles and lawless activities were common.

One of the best-known shoot-outs took place on October 26, 1881. It involved Wyatt Earp, a lawman in Tombstone, Arizona. That afternoon, Earp headed to Tombstone's OK Corral with his brothers Virgil and Morgan. Also with them was friend John Henry "Doc" Holliday. At the corral, the men faced a gang of **bandits**. After a fierce gun battle, three bandits lay dead in the street. Wyatt Earp was the only man not hit by a bullet.

MAY 6, 1882

Congress passes the Chinese Exclusion Act. This law stops Chinese **immigration** into the United States for the next 10 years.

JULY 14, 1881

"Wild West" outlaw William H. Bonney meets his end. So-called Billy the Kid is shot dead by Sheriff Pat Garrett at Fort Sumner in the New Mexico territory.

| 1803–1812 | 1819–1820 | 1820–1823 | 1830–1839 | 1844–1847 | 1845–1852 |

SEPTEMBER 5, 1882

After 19 years of construction, the Northern Pacific Railroad is completed. The line stretches west from the Great Lakes to the Pacific Ocean.

MARCH 1, 1886

Apache leader Geronimo surrenders to U.S. general Nelson A. Miles in Sonora, Mexico. Geronimo fought more than 30 years to save his Arizona homeland. He was the last American Indian chief to be defeated by U.S. forces. After surrendering, Geronimo is forced to resettle in Florida.

WINTER 1886–1887

An unusually harsh winter kills millions of cattle on the United States northern plains. With nothing to eat, more than 50 percent of all herds die of starvation or freeze to death. Ranchers later call the terrible season "the Great Die-up."

Harassment and Conflict

By the late 1880s, ranching was a big business in the new West. Many wealthy businessmen owned large cattle herds. **Cattle rustling** was a big problem on the **range**. The "cattle barons" often accused smaller, independent ranchers of stealing **livestock** from them.

The conflict reached its breaking point in April 1892. Several of the most powerful barons rode to Johnson County near Buffalo, Wyoming. They had a list of small ranchers they planned to kill. The barons brought 23 "hired guns" with them. Some of their important employees came as well.

The Johnson County War got quickly out of hand. Months of **harassment** and murder followed. Finally, the local government stepped in. Several of the cattle barons and their associates were arrested. None were ever brought to trial.

THE BATTLE AT Wounded Knee was the last major conflict between the U.S. Army and the Sioux Indians.

1803–1812   1819–1820   1820–1823   1830–1839   1844–1847   1845–1852

Massacre at Wounded Knee

On December 29, 1890, a fierce battle broke out at Wounded Knee Creek in South Dakota.

The conflict began when a gun went off as U.S. forces **disarmed** a group of Sioux American Indians. This accidental shot triggered a **massacre**. About 300 Sioux men, women, and children were killed within a few minutes. Sioux Chief Big Foot was among them.

SHEEPHERDERS WERE ALSO victims of the western range wars. They sometimes battled cattlemen to the death over grazing rights.

MASSACRE BY THE NUMBERS

Number of
U.S. troops
  500
Number of deaths
  25

Sioux left alive
  27
The U.S. government
reported only 126 deaths
  64 men
  44 women and girls
  18 babies

Turn of the Century

The early 1900s offered Americans many opportunities. Westward expansion made vast **natural resources** available. By 1900, the country was the world's largest steel producer. It had also become a world leader in agriculture.

On the West Coast, Americans established ports for shipping goods and resources by water. This led to greater trade with foreign markets in Asia and elsewhere. Artists and other creative people also migrated west. Many were drawn to the small town of Hollywood, California. There, the new art of moviemaking was finding a home.

Across the country, the turn of the century was an exciting time. It was also a period of great challenge and enormous growth. The nation's **Founding Fathers** had imagined a great future for their country. Now, that future had arrived. The United States was ready to show its power in a modern world.

MANY FILMMAKERS MOVED from New York to Hollywood due to the good weather there.

BY 1900, THE United States was producing 10 million tons (9 million metric tons) of steel every year.

"American history has been in a large degree the history of the colonization of the Great West."
Historian Frederick J. Turner, 1893

IN 1900, THE port of New Orleans was one of the world's largest shipping centers. Farther west, the California Shipping Company had more sailing ships than any other company in the world.

IN 1892, HENRY Ford built his first gasoline-fueled car, or "horseless carriage." He founded the Ford Motor Company in 1903. His was the first company to produce cars on an assembly line. The age of the automobile was on the horizon.

Activity

Fill in the Blanks

Timelines are only a beginning. They provide an overview of the key events and important people that shaped history. Now, discover more about westward expansion by researching in printed materials and on the internet.

A concept web can help organize your ideas. Use the questions in the concept web to guide your research. When finished, use the completed web to help you write a report.

"WILD WEST" BECAME a common term for a reason. As more people moved into unsettled areas, frontier towns grew. Few of these towns had any form of government. This led to crime and chaos.

Concept Web

Key People
- Discuss one or two main figures who had an impact on the times, event, or person you are researching.
- What negative or positive actions by people had a lasting effect on history?

Important Events
- What significant events shaped the times or the person you're writing about?
- Were there any major events that triggered some turning point in the life or the time you are writing about?

Historic Places
- Discuss some of the most important places related to the subject of your research.
- Are there some important places that are not well-known today?
- If so, what are they and why were they important at the time or to your subject?

Causes
- How was your subject affected by important historical moments of the time?
- Was there any chain of events to cause a particular outcome in the event, time, or the life you are researching?

Write a History Report

Obstacles
- What were some of the most difficult moments or events in the life of the person or in the historical timeline of the topic you are researching?
- Were there any particular people who greatly aided in the overcoming of obstacles?

Outcome and Lasting Effects
- What was the outcome of this chain of events?
- Was there a lasting effect on your subject?
- What is the importance of these "stepping stones" of history? How might the outcome have changed if things had happened differently?

Into the Future
- What lasting impact did your subject have on history?
- Is that person, time, or event well-known today?
- Have people's attitudes changed from back then until now about your subject?
- Do people think differently today about the subject than they did at the time the event happened or the person was alive?

Brain Teaser

1. Where was the last major battle between American forces and the Sioux Indians?

2. What year was the Missouri Compromise passed?

3. What were Lewis and Clark looking for in the Pacific Northwest?

4. When was the Monroe Doctrine announced?

5. What boundary line did the United States and Great Britain argue over in the 1840s?

6. How big was the Louisiana Purchase?

7. When did Congress pass the Kansas-Nebraska Act?

8. What state did the United States and Mexico fight over in the Mexican-American War?

9. What was the full name of the Wild West outlaw known as "Billy the Kid"?

10. In what year was the Ford Motor Company founded?

11. Who signed the Indian Removal Act into law in 1830?

12. When was the California gold rush at its height?

Key Words

49th parallel: an imaginary line 49 degrees north of the equator

annexed: added a territory to an existing territory

bandits: robbers, often a gang

cattle rustling: the theft of cows, bulls, or oxen

colonization: a country's building of settlements on foreign land

compromise: a settlement in which both sides give up something

disarmed: took weapons away from

expansion: growth or an increase in size

Founding Fathers: men who started the U.S. government and wrote the U.S. Constitution

frontier: a region at the edge of or beyond a settled area

harassment: repeated annoying or attacking behavior

immigration: the movement of people to another country or region

livestock: farm animals

massacre: the sudden and brutal killing of many

natural resources: materials that bring in money

pioneers: first people to explore or settle an unknown area

range: wide, open land for animal grazing

reservations: land reserved for use by American Indians

seceded: broke away

transcontinental: crossing a continent

treaty: a formal written promise or agreement

Union: another name for the United States, used mostly before and during the Civil War

Index

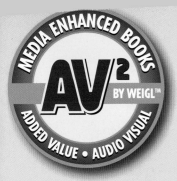

Log on to www.av2books.com

AV[2] by Weigl brings you media enhanced books that support active learning. Go to www.av2books.com, and enter the special code found on page 2 of this book. You will gain access to enriched and enhanced content that supplements and complements this book. Content includes video, audio, weblinks, quizzes, a slide show, and activities.

AV[2] Online Navigation

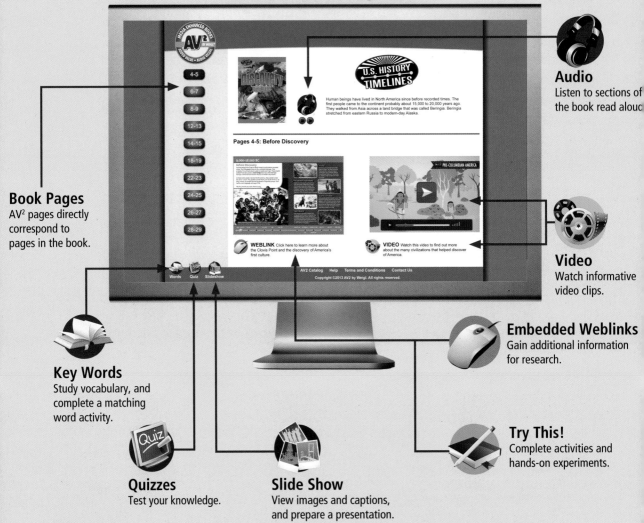

Audio
Listen to sections of the book read aloud

Book Pages
AV[2] pages directly correspond to pages in the book.

Video
Watch informative video clips.

Key Words
Study vocabulary, and complete a matching word activity.

Embedded Weblinks
Gain additional information for research.

Quizzes
Test your knowledge.

Slide Show
View images and captions, and prepare a presentation.

Try This!
Complete activities and hands-on experiments.

AV[2] was built to bridge the gap between print and digital. We encourage you to tell us what you like and what you want to see in the future.

Sign up to be an AV[2] Ambassador at www.av2books.com/ambassador.